# First World War
and Army of Occupation
# War Diary
France, Belgium and Germany

38 DIVISION
Divisional Troops
120 Brigade Royal Field Artillery
24 December 1915 - 29 August 1916

WO95/2546/2

The Naval & Military Press Ltd
www.nmarchive.com
Published in association with The National Archives

Published by

## The Naval & Military Press Ltd

Unit 10 Ridgewood Industrial Park,

Uckfield, East Sussex,

TN22 5QE England

Tel: +44 (0) 1825 749494

www.naval-military-press.com

www.nmarchive.com

*This diary has been reprinted in facsimile from the original. Any imperfections are inevitably reproduced and the quality may fall short of modern type and cartographic standards.*

© **Crown Copyright**
**Images reproduced by permission of The National Archives, London, England, 2015.**

# Contents

| Document type | Place/Title | Date From | Date To |
|---|---|---|---|
| Heading | WO95/2546/2 | | |
| Heading | 38th Division Divl Artillery 120th Brigade R.F.A. Dec 1915-Aug 1916. Bde. Broken UP | | |
| War Diary | Southampton | 24/12/1915 | 24/12/1915 |
| War Diary | Le Havre | 25/12/1915 | 26/12/1915 |
| War Diary | Merville | 27/12/1915 | 27/12/1915 |
| War Diary | Haverskerque | 28/12/1915 | 28/01/1916 |
| War Diary | Leslobes | 29/01/1916 | 29/02/1916 |
| Heading | 120th Bde. R.F.A. Vol. I Dec. 15 Aug. 16 | | |
| Heading | 120th Bde. A.C. Vol. 1, 2, 3 | | |
| Heading | War Diary Of 120th Brigade R.F.A. From:- December 24th 1915 To-January 31st 1916 (Volume.1 Sheet.3.) | | |
| War Diary | Winchester | 24/12/1915 | 24/12/1915 |
| War Diary | Southampton | 24/12/1915 | 24/12/1915 |
| War Diary | La Havre | 25/12/1915 | 26/12/1915 |
| War Diary | Lestrum | 26/12/1915 | 26/12/1915 |
| War Diary | Haverskerque | 26/12/1915 | 26/12/1915 |
| War Diary | Merville | 27/12/1915 | 27/12/1915 |
| War Diary | Lestrum | 27/12/1915 | 27/12/1915 |
| War Diary | Haverskerque | 27/12/1915 | 27/12/1915 |
| War Diary | Lestrum | 27/12/1915 | 27/12/1915 |
| War Diary | Merville | 27/12/1915 | 27/12/1915 |
| War Diary | Haverskerque | 28/12/1915 | 20/01/1916 |
| War Diary | Haverskerque | 00/01/1916 | 15/01/1916 |
| War Diary | Haverskerque | 14/01/1916 | 24/01/1916 |
| War Diary | Haverskerque | 23/01/1916 | 23/01/1916 |
| War Diary | Lacoutre | 31/01/1916 | 31/01/1916 |
| Heading | 120th Bde. R.F.A. Vol. 2 | | |
| War Diary | Lacouture. | 01/02/1916 | 29/02/1916 |
| Heading | 120 R.F.A. Vol 3 | | |
| War Diary | Lacouture. | 01/03/1916 | 15/04/1916 |
| War Diary | Laventie | 16/02/1916 | 10/05/1916 |
| War Diary | Merville. | 23/05/1916 | 27/05/1916 |
| War Diary | Laventie. | 01/05/1916 | 10/05/1916 |
| War Diary | Merville. | 23/05/1916 | 30/06/1916 |
| War Diary | Merville | 01/06/1916 | 30/06/1916 |
| War Diary | Perregot. | 01/07/1916 | 01/07/1916 |
| War Diary | Toutencourt. | 02/07/1916 | 03/07/1916 |
| War Diary | Treux Wood. | 04/07/1916 | 09/07/1916 |
| War Diary | Between Mametz & Carnoy. | 10/07/1916 | 18/07/1916 |
| War Diary | Meaulte. | 19/07/1916 | 19/07/1916 |
| War Diary | Courcelles | 20/07/1916 | 07/08/1916 |
| War Diary | Authie | 08/08/1916 | 09/08/1916 |
| War Diary | Hem | 10/08/1916 | 13/08/1916 |
| War Diary | Arneke | 14/08/1916 | 20/08/1916 |
| War Diary | Brielen & Poperinghe | 21/08/1916 | 25/08/1916 |
| War Diary | Poperinghe | 26/08/1916 | 29/08/1916 |

WO95/25462

## 38TH DIVISION
## DIVL ARTILLERY

120TH BRIGADE R.F.A.
DEC 1915 – AUG 1916.

BDE BROKEN UP

# WAR DIARY or INTELLIGENCE SUMMARY

Army Form C. 2118

120th Brigade R.F. Army Ammn. Column

24th to 31st Dec. 1915.

| Place | Date | Hour | Summary of Events and Information | Remarks and references to Appendices |
|---|---|---|---|---|
| SOUTHAMPTON | 24/12/15 | 2/5pm | Embarked on Transport S.S. "CITY OF DUNKIRK" for active service in France. Strength 4 Officers 161 other ranks 209 Horses. Names of Officers CAPTAIN E. PAVEY. 2Lieuts R.K.GREEN, G.M.AYERS and F.R. SMITH. | |
| LE HAVRE | 25/12/15 | 11am | Disembarked and proceeded to DOCKS BASE CAMP. LE HAVRE (Casualties on Voyage. 2 Horses destroyed.) (N°s 46 & 47) 4 Remounts posted to complete Est. | |
| -"- | 26/12/15 | 7pm | Entrained for MERVILLE. | |
| MERVILLE | 27/12/15 | 7pm | Detrained and proceeded by march route to billets at HAVERSKERQUE. | |
| HAVERSKERQUE | 28/12/15 | | In billets | |
| -"- | 29/12/15 | | -do- | |
| -"- | 30/12/15 | | -do- | |
| -"- | 31/12/15 | | -do- | |

F. Pavey Capt R.F.A.
Commdg 120th Bde R.F.A.
Ammn. Col.

Army Form C. 2118

# WAR DIARY
## or
## INTELLIGENCE SUMMARY 120th Bde R.F.A. Amm: Column
(Erase heading not required.)

1st to 24th Jan 1916

| Place | Date | Hour | Summary of Events and Information | Remarks and references to Appendices |
|---|---|---|---|---|
| HAVERSKERQUE | 1 | | In billets, work of improving horse standings and mens billets continued | |
| " | 2 | | No change | |
| " | 3 | | " " | |
| " | 4 | | " " | |
| " | 5 | | " " | |
| " | 6 | | " " | |
| " | 7 | | " " | |
| " | 8 | | " " | |
| " | 9 | | " " | Horse 811 evacuated |
| " | 10 | | " " | |
| " | 11 | | " " | |
| " | 12 | | " " | |
| " | 13 | | " " | |
| " | 14 | | " " | |
| " | 15 | | " " | Horse No 38 died |
| " | 16 | | " " | |
| " | 17 | | " " | |
| " | 18 | | " " | |
| " | 19 | | " " | |
| " | 20 | | " " | |
| " | 21 | | " " | |
| " | 22 | | " " | |
| " | 23 | | " " | |
| " | 24 | | " " | Horses Nos 15 & 19 evacuated |

Army Form C. 2118

# WAR DIARY
## or
## INTELLIGENCE SUMMARY

120th Bde. R.F.A. Amm. Column.

(Erase heading not required.)

Instructions regarding War Diaries and Intelligence Summaries are contained in F.S. Regs., Part II. and the Staff Manual respectively. Title Pages will be prepared in manuscript.

25th to 31st Jan 1916

| Place | Date | Hour | Summary of Events and Information | Remarks and references to Appendices |
|---|---|---|---|---|
| HAVERSKERQUE | 25/1/16 | | In billets. Supply of S.A.A. to Infy Bde 114th Infantry Bde commenced. | |
| " | 26 " | | " | |
| " | 27 " | | " | |
| " | 28 " | | " | |
| LES LOBES | 29 " | | Left half of B.A.C. moved to LES LOBES, via MERVILLE & LESTREM & took up billets vacated by 88th B.A.C. | |
| " | 30 " | | Right half of B.A.C. " " " " via ST VENANT. | |
| " | 31 " | | In billets. Supply of 18pr R.F. Amn to Batteries 120th Bde R.F.A. Commenced. | |

F. Parey Capt. R.F.A.
for in chg 120th Bde R.F.A. Amn Col.

Army Form C. 2118

# WAR DIARY
## or
## INTELLIGENCE SUMMARY  120th Bde R.F.A Amm: Column

1st to 29th Feb 1916

(Erase heading not required.)

Instructions regarding War Diaries and Intelligence Summaries are contained in F. S. Regs., Part II. and the Staff Manual respectively. Title Pages will be prepared in manuscript.

| Place | Date | Hour | Summary of Events and Information | Remarks and references to Appendices |
|---|---|---|---|---|
| LES LOBES | 1 |  | Sn Fill to Supply of QF Amn & Battries 120th Bde R.F.A. and S.A.A. to Bns & 119th Inf. Bde. continued. |  |
| " | 2 |  | " | LIEUT. J.S. ARNOLD joined. |
| " | 3 |  | " | Horse N° 30 destroyed. |
| " | 4 |  | " |  |
| " | 5 |  | " |  |
| " | 6 |  | " |  |
| " | 7 |  | " |  |
| " | 8 |  | " |  |
| " | 9 |  | " |  |
| " | 10 |  | " |  |
| " | 11 |  | " |  |
| " | 12 |  | " |  |
| " | 13 |  | " | 5" Remounts joined Telephl. Lt |
| " | 14 |  | " |  |
| " | 15 |  | " |  |
| " | 16 |  | " |  |
| " | 17 |  | " |  |
| " | 18 |  | " |  |
| " | 19 |  | " |  |
| " | 20 |  | " |  |
| " | 21 |  | " |  |
| " | 22 |  | " |  |
| " | 23 |  | " |  |
| " | 24 |  | " |  |
| " | 25 |  | " |  |
| " | 26 |  | " |  |
| " | 27 |  | " |  |
| " | 28 |  | " |  |
| " | 29 |  | " |  |

F Powel Capt R.F.A.
Comdg 120th Bde R.F.A.

120ᵗʰ Rec. NZ.
Vol I

Dec '15
Aug '16

120th Bde: A.C.
Vols: 1,2,3

# CONFIDENTIAL
## WAR DIARY
### OF
### 120th BRIGADE R.F.A.

From:- December 24th 1915 To:- January 31st 1916

(Volume .1.
Sheets .3.)

Army Form C. 2118.

# WAR DIARY
## INTELLIGENCE SUMMARY.
*(Erase heading not required.)*

December 1915.

120th Brigade R.F.A.

| Place | Date | Hour | Summary of Events and Information | Remarks and references to Appendices |
|---|---|---|---|---|
| Winchester | 23/12/15 | | Left Winchester for Southampton by road. | |
| Southampton | 24/12/15 | 10 a.m. 10 to 2 p.m. | Unit arrived at Southampton Docks. | |
| Southampton | 24/12/15 | 4 p.m. to 8 p.m. | Unit left Southampton in 2 transports for Le Havre. | |
| Le Havre | 25/12/15 | 10 a.m. | Arrived at disembarkation sheds, Le Havre Docks. | |
| Le Havre | 25/12/15 | 9 p.m. | Headquarters Staff, A and B Batteries entrained for Merville and Lilium. C and D Batteries and Brigade Ammunition Column at No 3. Rest Camp, Le Havre. | |
| Le Havre | 26/12/15 | 12 noon | 'C' Battery entrained for Lilium. | |
| Le Havre | 26/12/15 | 4 p.m. | 'D' Battery entrained for Lilium. | |
| Le Havre | 26/12/15 | 9.30 p.m. | Brigade Ammunition Column entrained for Merville. | |
| Lilium | 26/12/15 | 10.30 p.m. | Headquarters Staff and 'A' Battery arrived Lilium. | |

Crawford L? R.F.A. Lt Col
O.C. Brigade R.F.A.

Army Form C. 2118.

# WAR DIARY
## or
## INTELLIGENCE SUMMARY.
*(Erase heading not required.)*

November 1915. 120th Brigade R.F.A.

Instructions regarding War Diaries and Intelligence Summaries are contained in F. S. Regs., Part II. and the Staff Manual respectively. Title pages will be prepared in manuscript.

| Place | Date | Hour | Summary of Events and Information | Remarks and references to Appendices |
|---|---|---|---|---|
| Haverskerque | 26/12/15 | Midnight | Headquarters Staff and 'A' Battery arrived Haverskerque. | |
| Merville | 27/12/15 | 2. a.m. | 'B' Battery billeted at Merville. | |
| Lestrem | 27/12/15 | 10. a.m. | 'C' Battery arrived Lestrem and detrained | |
| Haverskerque | 27/12/15 | 1 p.m. | 'B' Battery arrived at Haverskerque. | |
| do. | 27/12/15 | 2 p.m. | 'C' Battery arrived at Haverskerque. | |
| Lestrem | 27/12/15 | 4.30 p.m. | 'D' Battery arrived Lestrem and detrained | |
| Merville | 27/12/15 | 9.30 p.m. | Brigade Ammunition Column arrived Merville and detrained | |
| Haverskerque | Midnight | | 'D' Battery arrived Haverskerque | |
| do. | 28/12/15 | 2. a.m. | Brigade Ammunition Column arrived at Haverskerque | |
| do. | 31/12/15 | | Brigade in rest at Busnes. | |

Ansuyas ?, R.F.A. for Adjt,
120th Brigade R.F.A.

January 1916.

# WAR DIARY

## INTELLIGENCE SUMMARY.
(Erase heading not required.)

120th Brigade R.F.A.  Army Form C. 2118.

| Place | Date | Hour | Summary of Events and Information | Remarks and references to Appendices |
|---|---|---|---|---|
| Source Anzac during the month on various days | | | Detachments from the Batteries dropped up to the firing line, Rookery taking over the Guns of the 88th Brigade R.F.A. | |
| Mudros | 2/1/16 | | A.Q. Major A. Wallace. A/Battery invalided from pneumonia, leaving Lemnos to Base 11/1/16. discharged. 32nd | |
| do. | 10/1/16 | | 2/Lt S.H.O. King joined and posted to 'A' Battery | |
| do. | 15/1/16 | | A/Bombardier T. Matthews B/Battery died of pneumonia. | |
| do. | 14/1/16 | | 2/Lt J.H. Turner joined and posted to 'B' Battery | |
| do. | 23/1/16 | | No. 56.25 Dr J.H. Heal wounded by shrapnel. 15/1/16 | |
| do. | 24/1/16 | | I.M.B.O. embarked in Hospital Ship for England. { 2/Lt H.T. Grench joined and posted { to 'B' Battery 15/1/16 } |
| do. | 23/1/16 | | 1 man do. | |
| Lemnos | 31/1/16 | | 1 Howitzer taken in Charge of the Brigade. Brigade took over Guns and position of 88th Brigade R.F.A. | Employed F.R.A. for duty 120th Brigade R.F.A. |

120× Box R.I.Q.
Vol. 2

Army Form C. 2118

# WAR DIARY
## or
## INTELLIGENCE SUMMARY

(Erase heading not required.)

120TH BRIGADE. R.F.A.

FEBRUARY 1916.

Instructions regarding War Diaries and Intelligence Summaries are contained in F.S. Regs., Part II. and the Staff Manual respectively. Title Pages will be prepared in manuscript.

| Place | Date | Hour | Summary of Events and Information | Remarks and references to Appendices |
|---|---|---|---|---|
| Lacouture. | 1/2/16 | | Group formed - Right Group, 38th Divisional Artillery, with the following batteries:- A, B, C, D/120 Brigade R.F.A, A/121, and C/122 Brigade (Hows) and C/119 (sec) (enfilade guns). | |
| " | 1/2/16 | 12 noon. | Wire cutting operation by C/120 South of Ferme-du-bois, remaining batteries firing on their respective zones. | |
| " | 2/2/16 | 1 p.m. | A/120 and A/121 minor operation in conjunction with Trench Mortars. | |
| " | 5/2/16 | 3 pm. | A/120 and A/121 in conjunction with Trench Mortar Battery on enemy's parapet. | |
| " | 6/2/16 | 2/45 pm. | A/120 (enfilade gun), B/120 and C/120. Enemy trench bombarded. | |
| " | 10/2/16 | 3/15 pm. | Suspected Enemy O.P. engaged by B/120. | |
| " | 11/2/16 | 2/15 pm. | "      "      "      "      C/122. | |
| " | 12/2/16 | | Test co-operation between Infantry and Artillery for retaliation carried out by A/120, B/120, C/120. | |
| " | 13/2/16 | 3.5 | Minor scheme. Trenches behind Fme Cour-d-Avoue engaged by B/120, C/120, and D/120. | |
| " | 15/2/16 | | Group re-arranged :- A/120, A/121, C/120, and D/120., left Right Group, 38th Div. Artillery, replaced by following Batteries:- B/87 and D/87. | |
| " | 16/2/16 | | Group becomes Left Group, 38th Div. Art. comprising:- B/120, C/122, B/87 and D/87 and C/119 ( Sec. enfilade ). | |
| " | 17/2/16 | 3/30 pm. | B/87 engage Enemy Front line and support trenches in conjunction with Trench Mortars. | |

Army Form C. 2118

# WAR DIARY
## or
## INTELLIGENCE SUMMARY
(Erase heading not required.)

120TH BRIGADE. R.F.A. (contd).

FEBRUARY 1916.

Instructions regarding War Diaries and Intelligence Summaries are contained in F.S. Regs., Part II. and the Staff Manual respectively. Title Pages will be prepared in manuscript.

| Place | Date | Hour | Summary of Events and Information | Remarks and references to Appendices |
|---|---|---|---|---|
| Lacouture. | 20/2/16 | 9/45 pm. | Test Gas Alarm sounded. Batteries prepared for action, orders to stand down received 10/45pm. | |
| " | 21/2/16 | " | "X" and "V" R.H.A. relieved B/87 and D/87. | |
| " | 23/2/16 | 9/20 pm. | B/120 engaged enemy's communication trenches. | |
| " | 26/2/16 | 2/30 | "X" and "V" R.H.A. with Trench Mortars engaged enemy's support trenches. | |
| " | 28/2/16 | | Artillery Test by "X". "V" R.H.A. and B/120., in answer to retaliation call by Infantry on enemy's parapet. | |
| " | 29/2/16 | 5.30 pm. | "X" R.H.A. with Trench Mortars engaged Boars Head. | |

C. Mayne Lt. R.F.A. for Lt. Col.
Commdg. 120. Brigade R.F.A.

38

120 RFA
Vol 3

Army Form C. 2118

# WAR DIARY
## ~~INTELLIGENCE SUMMARY~~
*(Erase heading not required.)*

120TH BRIGADE R.F.A.

MARCH 1916.

Instructions regarding War Diaries and Intelligence Summaries are contained in F.S. Regs., Part II. and the Staff Manual respectively. Title Pages will be prepared in manuscript.

| Place | Date | Hour | Summary of Events and Information | Remarks and references to Appendices |
|---|---|---|---|---|
| Lacouture. | March 1916. -1st | | | |
| " | -1st | | Detachments of 35th D.A. attached for instructional purposes. Group now becomes- Right Group, 19th Div. Artillery. | |
| " | -2nd | | | |
| " | -3rd | | "X" and "V" R.H.A. minor operation in conjunction with Trench Mortars. | |
| " | -4th | | | |
| " | -5th | | | |
| " | -6th | | | |
| " | -7th | | | |
| " | -8th | | Group becomes 35th. Div. Artillery Group under command of O.C. 120th Brigade R.F.A. 38th Div. Art. "C"/157 relieve "V" R.H.A. "D"/157 relieve "X" R.H.A. Batteries now in Group as follows:- "B"/120, "C"/122, "C"/119(Section for enfilade purposes), "C"/157 and "D"/157. | |
| " | -9th | | | |
| " | -10th | | | |
| " | -11th | | Artillery Test for new Batteries in reply to call for retaliation by Infantry. | |
| " | -12th | | Same as on the 11th inst. | |
| " | -13th | | More Artillery Tests. "B"/120 engage Snipers post with 70 rounds at request of Infantry, who report same to be effective. | |

1875 Wt. W593/826 1,000,000 4/15 J.B.C. & A. A.D.S.S./Forms/C. 2118.

Army Form C. 2118

No. 2.

# WAR DIARY

## INTELLIGENCE SUMMARY

*(Erase heading not required.)*

MARCH 1916 (contd).

Instructions regarding War Diaries and Intelligence Summaries are contained in F. S. Regs., Part II. and the Staff Manual respectively. Title Pages will be prepared in manuscript.

| Place | Date | Hour | Summary of Events and Information | Remarks and references to Appendices |
|---|---|---|---|---|
| Lacouture. | March 1916. -14th- | 7-30 a.m. | 2 Detachments of "H" R.H.A., with section of guns from "B"/158., engage in wire cutting operation - 199 rounds. | |
| " | -15th- | | "D"/157 engage enemy's front line at request of Infantry in retaliation for rifle grenades. | |
| " | -16th- | | "C"/163(Hows) come into the Group. "B"/120, "C"/157, "D"/157 and "C"/122, engage enemy's front line in conjunction with Trench mortars. Enfilade section wire cutting operation - 220 rounds. | |
| " | -17th- | | Registering. | |
| " | -18th- | | Registering. | |
| " | -19th- | | Registering. | |
| " | -20th- | | "C"/157 - 18 rounds at request of Infantry - retaliation. | |
| " | -21st- | | | |
| " | -22nd- | | "C"/157 and "D"/157, 150 rounds each, wire cutting operation, preparation for raid by Infantry. "B"/120 and "C"/122 withdraw ; relieved by "A"/157 and "D"/163. | |
| " | -23rd- | | "A"/157 - 50 rounds wire cutting operation. ("A"/157 and "C"/158 personnel) and "C"/163 withdraw from Group to billets near St.Venant. | |
| " | -24th- | | Infantry raid by 17th Battln Lanc's Fusiliers. No artillery support called for. | |

Army Form C. 2118

# WAR DIARY
## INTELLIGENCE SUMMARY
*(Erase heading not required.)*

No. 3.

MARCH 1916. (contd).

Instructions regarding War Diaries and Intelligence Summaries are contained in F.S. Regs., Part II. and the Staff Manual respectively. Title Pages will be prepared in manuscript.

| Place | Date | Hour | Summary of Events and Information | Remarks and references to Appendices |
|---|---|---|---|---|
| Lacouture. | March 1916. 25th. | | "A"/157 and "D"/163 withdraw, relieved by "B"/120 and "C"/122. "C"/157 and "D"/157 leave Group, relieved by 19th Division Batteries. "C"/157 and "D"/157 and "C"/122. Artillery under Command of 87th Brigade Headquarters, 1 battery of 120th Brigade remain in Group viz:- "B"/120. 120th Brigade Headquarters withdraw to billets in rear, near FOSSE. | |
| " | 26th. | | | |
| " | 27th. | | | |
| " | 28th. | | | |
| " | 29th. | | | |
| " | 30th. | | | |
| " | 31st. | | | |

Andrews L.?.A.? Lt. Col.
Commanding 120th Brigade R.F.A.

Army Form C. 2118

# WAR DIARY
## or
## INTELLIGENCE SUMMARY
*(Erase heading not required.)*

120TH BRIGADE. R.F.A.  Vol 4

APRIL 1916.

Instructions regarding War Diaries and Intelligence Summaries are contained in F.S. Regs., Part II. and the Staff Manual respectively. Title Pages will be prepared in manuscript.

| Place | Date | Hour | Summary of Events and Information | Remarks and references to Appendices |
|---|---|---|---|---|
| Lacouture. | April 1916. 1st | | 120th Brigade Headquarters in rest, billeted in rear near FOSSE. | |
| " | 14th | | Unit moved to LAVENTIE to relieve the 88th Brigade, 19th Div. Artillery. | |
| " | 15th | | "A", "B", "C" and "D" Batteries, 120th F.A. Brigade, together with "A" & "D" Batteries 122nd. How. Brigade, relieved corresponding F.A. and How Batteries of the 88th & 89th Brigades respectively., Left Group, 19th Div. Arty at LAVENTIE becoming the Right Group, of the 38th Div. Arty., under the Command of Lt.Col. C.O. Head. R.F.A., O.C. 120th Brigade R.F.A. | |
| Laventie | 16th | | Batteries engaged in Registration. | |
| " | 17th | | Registration and checking Zero Lines. | |
| " | 18th 19th 20th 21st 22nd 23rd 24th 25th 26th 27th 28th 29th 30th | | Ammunition limited, the Batteries were generally inactive and made little reply to the rather aggressive activity of the enemy. | |

1875 Wt. W593/826 1,000,000 4/15 I.R.C. & A. A.D.S.S./Forms/C. 2118.

Army Form C. 2118

XXXVIII Vol. 5

# WAR DIARY
## of
## INTELLIGENCE SUMMARY
(Erase heading not required.)

120TH. BRIGADE R.F.A.

MAY 1916.

Instructions regarding War Diaries and Intelligence Summaries are contained in F.S. Regs., Part II. and the Staff Manual respectively. Title Pages will be prepared in manuscript.

| Place | Date | Hour | Summary of Events and Information | Remarks and references to Appendices |
|---|---|---|---|---|
| Laventie. | May 1916. 1st to | | Brigade still in action East of Laventie. (Ammunition still limited - but by steady careful shooting more caution and regard for the consequences had been imposed on the enemy. | |
| " | -10th- to | | 120th. Brigade Head Quarters withdrew to billet in rear near LA GORGUE, handing over the Command of the Right Group, 38th. D.A. to the 122nd. Brigade Head Quarters - The Batteries remained at their positions in action. | |
| Merville. | -23rd- | | Head Quarters left its billets near LA GORGUE and took over billets at MERVILLE. | |
| " | -27th- | | The Brigade was re-organised - "B" Battery being transferred to the 122nd. Brigade and ("B"/122 (Hows) replacing it in the 120th. Brigade: - The B.A.C. was broken up, the greater part of it going to the D.A.C. and the balance to CALAIS. | |

E. Moad
Lt. Colonel. R.F.A.
Commanding 120th. Brigade. R.F.A.

Army Form C. 2118

# WAR DIARY
## of
## INTELLIGENCE SUMMARY
*(Erase heading not required.)*

120TH. BRIGADE R.F.A.

MAY 1916.

Instructions regarding War Diaries and Intelligence Summaries are contained in F. S. Regs., Part II. and the Staff Manual respectively. Title Pages will be prepared in manuscript.

| Place | Date | Hour | Summary of Events and Information | Remarks and references to Appendices |
|---|---|---|---|---|
| Laventie. | May 1916. -1st. to -10th- | | (Brigade still in action East of Laventie. (Ammunition still limited – but by steady careful shooting more caution and regard for the (consequences had been imposed on the enemy. | |
| " | -10th- to | | (120th. Brigade Head Quarters withdrew to billet in rear near LA GORGUE, handing over the (Command of the Right Group, 38th. D.A. to the 122nd. Brigade Head Quarters – The Batteries (remained at their positions in action. | |
| Merville. | -23rd- to | | Head Quarters left its billets near LA GORGUE and took over billets at MERVILLE. | |
| " | -27th- | | (The Brigade was re-organised – "B" Battery being transferred to the 122nd. Brigade and ("B"/122 (Hows) replacing it in the 120th. Brigade; – The B.A.C. was broken up, the greater (part of it going to the D.A.C. and the balance to CALAIS. | |

Lt.Colonel. R.F.A.

Commanding 120th. Brigade. R. F. A.

XXXVIII

Army Form C. 2118.

# WAR DIARY

## INTELLIGENCE SUMMARY.

(Erase heading not required.)

120th Brigade R.F.A.  June 1916.

| Place | Date | Hour | Summary of Events and Information | Remarks and references to Appendices |
|---|---|---|---|---|
| MERVILLE | June 1 | | Headquarters still in its billets at MERVILLE. | |
| | 2 | | | |
| | 3 | | | |
| | 4 | | | |
| | 5 | | | |
| | 6 | | Batteries in action East of LAVENTIE | |
| | 7 | | | |
| | 8 | | | |
| | 9 | | | |
| | 10 | | | |
| | 11 | | | |
| | 12 | | Brigade Headquarters marched to near AUBIGNY with "C" & "D" Batteries — "A" & "B" Batteries were | |
| | 13 | | withdrawn from the line and moved to a training area near ST. POL. | |
| | 14 | | | |
| | 15 | | | |

Sheet No. 2

# WAR DIARY
## ~~INTELLIGENCE~~ SUMMARY.
*(Erase heading not required.)*

Army Form C. 2118.

12th Brigade R.F.A.
June 1916.

| Place | Date | Hour | Summary of Events and Information | Remarks and references to Appendices |
|---|---|---|---|---|
| | 16. | | "C" & "D" Batteries went into action between SOUCHEZ and NEUVILLE St VAAST. | |
| | 17. | | | |
| | 18. | | Bde Hd Qrs moved to rejoin "A" & "B" Batteries in camp near ST. POL. | |
| | 19. | | | |
| | 20. | | ⎫ "A" & "B" Batteries | |
| | 21. | | ⎬ Battery & Brigade training — "C" & "D" Batteries still in action. | |
| | 22. | | ⎭ | |
| | 23. | | | |
| | 24. | | | |
| | 25. | | | |
| | 26. | | | |
| | 27. | | | |
| | 28. | | Bde Hd Qrs moved to ACQ near AUBIGNY. — "A" & "B" Batteries moved to Tillelois west of DOULLENS. | |
| | 29. | | | |
| | 30. | | Bde Hd Qrs & "C" & "D" Batteries moved to Tillelois 10 miles west of ALBERT. — "A" & "B" Batteries arrived at same place on the same day & the Brigade got together again. | |

E Meach O.C
2.7.16

Cmg 12) "B" R.F.A.

Army Form C. 2118.

# WAR DIARY
## or
## INTELLIGENCE SUMMARY. 120th Brigade R.F.A. June 1916
(Erase heading not required.)

Instructions regarding War Diaries and Intelligence Summaries are contained in F. S. Regs., Part II. and the Staff Manual respectively. Title pages will be prepared in manuscript.

| Place | Date | Hour | Summary of Events and Information | Remarks and references to Appendices |
|---|---|---|---|---|
| MERVILLE | June 1916 1 | | Headquarters still in the billets at MERVILLE | |
| | 2 | | | |
| | 3 | | | |
| | 4 | | | |
| | 5 | | | |
| | 6 | | Batteries in action East of LAVENTIE | |
| | 7 | | | |
| | 8 | | | |
| | 9 | | | |
| | 10 | | | |
| | 11 | | | |
| | 12 | | Brigade Headquarters marched to meet AUBIGNY with "C" & "D" Batteries - "A" & "B" | |
| | 13 | | Batteries were withdrawn from the line & marched to a training area near ST POL. | |
| | 14 | | | |
| | 15 | | | |
| | 16 | | | |

Sheet No 2

Army Form C. 2118.

# WAR DIARY
## or
## INTELLIGENCE SUMMARY.
(Erase heading not required.)

120th Brigade R.F.A.  June 1916

| Place | Date | Hour | Summary of Events and Information | Remarks and references to Appendices |
|---|---|---|---|---|
| | 17 | | "C" & "D" Batteries went into action between SOUCHEZ & NEUVILLE ST VAAST | |
| | 18 | | | |
| | 19 | | Brigade Headquarters moved to rejoin A & B Batteries in camp near ST POL. | |
| | 20 | | | |
| | 21 | | "A" & "B" Batteries | |
| | 22 | | Battery & Brigade training - "C" & "D" Batteries still in action | |
| | 23 | | | |
| | 24 | | | |
| | 25 | | | |
| | 26 | | | |
| | 27 | | | |
| | 28 | | Brigade Headquarters moved to ACQ near AUBIGNY | |
| | 29 | | "A" & "B" Batteries moved to billets West of DOULLENS. | |
| | 30 | | Brigade Headquarters & "C" & "D" Batteries moved to billets 10 miles West of ALBERT. "A" & "B" Batteries arrived at same place on the same day & the Brigade got together again | |

2.7.16

R Henry Lt Col
Comdg 120 Bde RFA

Army Form C. 2118.

# WAR DIARY
## of
## ~~INTELLIGENCE SUMMARY~~   120TH. BRIGADE R.F.A.

*(Erase heading not required.)*   JULY 1916.

| Place | Date | Hour | Summary of Events and Information | Remarks and references to Appendices |
|---|---|---|---|---|
| Perregot. | July. 1st. | 10pm. | Marched to TOUTENCOURT (8 miles), remained there 'till July 3rd. | |
| Toutencourt. | 2nd | | | |
| " | 3rd. | 7pm. | Marched to TREUX WOOD - 10 miles, bivouacked there 'till July 9th. Weather very bad, heavy rain and thunderstorms. | |
| Treux Wood. | 4th. | | | |
| " | 5th. | | | |
| " | 6th. | | | |
| " | 7th. | | | |
| " | 8th. | | | |
| " | 9th. | 7pm. | Went into action between MAMETZ & CARNOY. | |
| Between Mametz & Carnoy. | 10th. | | Engaged enemy trenches in front of BAZENTIN-LE-GRAND wood and enemy forces counter-attacking CONTALMAISON. | |
| " | 11th. | | "A", "B", "C" Batteries moved forward to a position near POMMIERS TRENCH. | |
| as above. | 11th. | | Engaged same targets as before, especially wire-cutting in front of BAZENTIN-LE-GRAND wood. | |
| In 2nd. | (12th. | | From subsequent examination not a strand of this wire was uncut | |
| position. | (13th. | | | |
| | (14th. | | on the 14th. | |
| As above. | 15th. | | Moved to 3rd position- 1,500 yards N.E. of MONTAUBAN, almost in ^original German 2nd line and only about 100 yards behind our own Infantry. | |

T2134. Wt. W708—776. 500000. 4/15. Sw J. C. & S.

Army Form C. 2118.

# WAR DIARY

## INTELLIGENCE SUMMARY. 120TH. BRIGADE R.F.A.

Sheet. No. 2.

*(Erase heading not required.)*

JULY 1916.

Instructions regarding War Diaries and Intelligence Summaries are contained in F. S. Regs., Part II. and the Staff Manual respectively. Title pages will be prepared in manuscript.

| Place | Date | Hour | Summary of Events and Information | Remarks and references to Appendices |
|---|---|---|---|---|
| In 3rd position. | July. 15th. 16th. 17th. 18th. | | We were shelled heavily by day and fired upon by machine guns at night, but had only five or six wounded. Our targets were usually the new German Trench and wire EAST & WEST of HIGH WOOD, and many small parties of the enemy seen moving on the opposite ridge, on whom we inflicted many casualties. | |
| 3rd position. | 18th. | 11-55 p.m. | The Brigade was withdrawn from its position and retired to its wagon lines at MEAULTE. Under fire this was rather a delicate operation, but was effected without loss. Owing to heavy rains and much traffic the tracks were in a dreadfully heavy state and the horses were much exhausted by the time they got back to the wagon lines. | |
| Meaulte. | 19th. | 3 p.m. | Marched to COUIN (18 miles). The horses not recovered from their previous exertions this march was slow and tedious. | |
| Courcelles | 20th. | | Moved into action EAST of COURCELLES with Hd. Qrs at latter place. The 120th Brigade R.F.A. and three Batteries 119th Bde formed the Right Group of the Division under command of Lt.Col. Head. Commanding 120th Bde R.F.A. | |
| " | 21st. 22nd. 23rd. 24th. | | ------------- ------------- ------------- ------------- | |
| " | 25th. | | In a re-organization of the Group, one Battery-"B"/119 was transferred to a group on our right and our group became the Centre Group. | |
| " | 26th. 27th. 28th. 29th. 30th. | | ------------- ------------- ------------- ------------- ------------- | |
| " | 31st. | | Still in action EAST of COURCELLES- no event of importance to relate. | |

Lt. Colonel. R.F.A.
Commanding 120th. Brigade. R. F. A.

Army Form C. 2118.

# WAR DIARY
## or
## INTELLIGENCE SUMMARY.

(Erase heading not required.)

120th. Brigade R.F.A.

August 1916.

Vol 8

| Place | Date | Hour | Summary of Events and Information | Remarks and references to Appendices |
|---|---|---|---|---|
| Courcelles | August 1st.–6th. | | In action East of Courcelles – no event of importance to relate. | |
| " | 7th. | | Group taken over by Guards Divisional Artillery. Units of 76th. Bde R.F.A. relieved corresponding units of 120th. Bde R.F.A. | |
| Authie | 8th. | | 120th. Bde moves to wagon lines in the vicenity of Authie. | |
| " | 9th. | | Still at Authie. | |
| Hem | 10th. | | 120th Brigade marched to and bivouaced at Hem. | |
| " | 11th. | | At Hem. | |
| " | 12th. | | At Hem. | |
| | 13th. | | Brigade entrained at Doullens and detrained at Cassel. Afterwards marched to alloted billets in VIIth. Corps Reserve Area near Arneke. | |
| Arneke | 14th. | | At Arneke. | |
| " | 15th. | | " | |
| " | 16th. | | " | |
| " | 17th. | | " | |
| " | 18th. | | " | |
| " | 19th. | | " | |
| " | 20th. | | " | |
| Brielen & Poperinghe | 21st. | | Personnel of batteries of Bde went up into the line near Brielen to relieve personnel of 4th. Divisional Batteries. Batteries were all in Right Group 38th Divisional Artillery. | |
| " | 22nd. | | 120th Brigade Headquarters moved/to billets in Poperinghe. | |
| " | 23rd. | | Batteries still in action near Brielen – no event of importance to relate. | |
| " | 24th. | | Brigade Headquarters still in billets at Poperinghe. | |
| " | 25th. | | " " " " " " " | |

Army Form C. 2118.

# WAR DIARY
Cont. Sheet No.2
or
## INTELLIGENCE SUMMARY. 120th. Brigade R.F.A.

August 1915

*(Erase heading not required.)*

| Place | Date | Hour | Summary of Events and Information | Remarks and references to Appendices |
|---|---|---|---|---|
| Poperinghe | 26th. | | Brigade Headquarters still in billets at Poperinghe. | |
| " | 27th. | | " " " " " " " | |
| " | 28th. | | " " " " " " " | |
| " | 29th. | | Owing to reorganization of Batteries into six gun batteries the 120th. Brigade was broken up and ceased to exist. | |


Lt.Colonel. R.F.A.
Commanding 120th. Brigade. R. F. A.

www.ingramcontent.com/pod-product-compliance
Lightning Source LLC
Chambersburg PA
CBHW081249170426
43191CB00037B/2094